Brazilian

Cooking

Introduction

Welcome to an enticing culinary voyage through the vibrant cuisine of Brazil. This captivating cookbook invites you to explore a world of rich and diverse flavors, where every page unveils the essence of this remarkable country. From the lively streets of Rio de Janeiro to the serene beaches of Bahia, immerse yourself in Brazil's remarkable food heritage, a reflection of its diverse landscapes and captivating population.

In these pages, you will discover a collection of authentic Brazilian recipes that showcase the unique blend of indigenous, African, and Portuguese influences that shape Brazil's culinary tapestry. Each recipe tells a story, reflecting the regional traditions, cultural celebrations, and the love for food that is deeply rooted in Brazilian culture.

Prepare to tantalize your taste buds with the vibrant and bold flavors that define Brazilian cuisine. From the fiery spices of the Northeast to the tropical fruits of the Amazon rainforest, every dish is a celebration of Brazil's abundance and diversity. Whether you are a seasoned cook or new to Brazilian cuisine, this cookbook offers something for everyone.

Explore the iconic dishes that have gained international acclaim, such as feijoada, the hearty black bean stew, and pão de queijo, the addictive cheese bread. Delight in the delicate flavors of seafood in moqueca de peixe, or savor the comforting embrace of a creamy brigadeiro. From savory to sweet, street food to festive feasts, we have curated a selection of recipes that will transport you to the heart of Brazil's culinary soul.

So, grab your apron, embrace the rhythmic beats of samba, and get ready to embark on a mouthwatering culinary journey through Brazil.

Feijoada

Brazil's national dish, a hearty black bean stew with various cuts of pork, beef, and sausages.

Ingredients:

1 lb black beans (soaked overnight)
1 lb mixed meats (such as pork ribs, smoked sausage, bacon, and beef)
1 large onion, chopped
4 cloves of garlic, minced
2 bay leaves
2 tbsps. vegetable oil
Salt and pepper to taste
Farofa (toasted cassava flour) for serving
Rice for serving
Orange slices for garnish

Directions:

1. Drain and rinse the soaked black beans. In a large pot, add the beans and cover them with water. Bring to a boil and cook until the beans are tender (approximately 1-2 hours). Drain and set aside.
2. In a separate large pot, heat the vegetable oil over medium heat.
3. Add the chopped onion and minced garlic, sautéing until they become fragrant and translucent.
4. Add the mixed meats (pork ribs, smoked sausage, bacon, and beef) to the pot.
5. Cook until the meats are browned and cooked through.
6. Add the cooked black beans to the pot with the meats.
7. Stir in the bay leaves and season with salt and pepper to taste.
8. Add enough water to cover the mixture.
9. Reduce the heat to low and let the feijoada simmer for at least 1 hour, allowing the flavors to meld together.
10. Stir occasionally and add more water if needed to maintain a stew-like consistency.

11. Serve the feijoada hot with rice, farofa, and orange slices as garnish.

Farofa

A toasted cassava or cornmeal mixture cooked with butter, onions, and various seasonings, often served as a side dish.

Ingredients:

1 cup cassava flour (also known as farinha de mandioca or yuca flour)
4 tbsps. butter or oil
1 small onion, finely chopped
2 cloves of garlic, minced
Salt and pepper to taste
Optional: diced bacon, cooked and crumbled (around 1/4 cup)

Directions:

1. Heat a large skillet or frying pan over medium heat.
2. Add the butter or oil to the pan and let it melt.
3. Add the chopped onion and minced garlic to the pan. Sauté until the onion becomes translucent and the garlic is fragrant.
4. If using diced bacon, add it to the pan and cook until it becomes crispy and browned.
5. Gradually add the cassava flour to the pan, stirring continuously to ensure it is evenly coated with the butter or oil mixture.
6. Cook for about 5-7 minutes, or until the flour turns golden brown and becomes crispy.
7. Season with salt and pepper to taste. Remember to taste and adjust the seasoning as needed.
8. Remove the pan from heat and let the farofa cool slightly before serving.
9. Serve the farofa as a side dish alongside feijoada, grilled meats, or other Brazilian dishes.

Coxinha

Deep-fried chicken croquettes with a creamy filling, typically made with shredded chicken and cream cheese.

Ingredients:

For the dough:
2 cups cooked and shredded chicken breast
2 cups chicken broth
2 tbsps. butter
2 cups all-purpose flour
1 cup milk
Salt to taste
For the filling:
1 cup cooked and shredded chicken breast
1 small onion, finely chopped
2 cloves of garlic, minced
2 tbsps. olive oil
1/2 cup cream cheese
Salt and pepper to taste
For breading and frying:
2 eggs, beaten
2 cups breadcrumbs
Oil for frying

Directions:

1. In a large saucepan, melt the butter over medium heat.
2. Add the flour and cook for a few minutes, stirring constantly, to make a roux.
3. Gradually add the chicken broth and milk to the saucepan, stirring continuously to avoid lumps.
4. Cook until the mixture thickens and forms a dough-like consistency.
5. Remove the dough from the heat and let it cool slightly.
6. Add the cooked and shredded chicken breast to the dough, season with salt, and mix well.
7. In a separate skillet, heat the olive oil over medium heat.

8. Add the chopped onion and minced garlic, sautéing until they become translucent.
9. Add the cooked and shredded chicken breast to the skillet. Season with salt and pepper, and cook for a few minutes to allow the flavors to blend together. Remove from heat and let the filling cool.
10. Take a small portion of the dough and flatten it in your hand. Place a tsp. of the filling in the center of the dough and shape it into a cone, sealing the edges to enclose the filling. Repeat with the remaining dough and filling.
11. Dip each coxinha into the beaten eggs, then roll it in breadcrumbs to coat evenly.
12. Heat oil in a deep pan or fryer to about 350°F (175°C). Fry the coxinhas in batches until they turn golden brown and crispy. Remove with a slotted spoon and place them on paper towels to drain excess oil.
13. Serve the coxinhas warm as a delicious snack or appetizer.

Pão de Queijo

Chewy and cheesy bread rolls made with tapioca flour and cheese, often served as a snack or breakfast item.

Ingredients:

2 cups tapioca flour/starch
1 cup milk
1/2 cup vegetable oil
2 eggs
1 tsp. salt
1 cup grated cheese (traditionally, use Brazilian Minas cheese or Parmesan cheese)

Directions:

1. Preheat your oven to 375°F (190°C). Grease a baking sheet or line it with parchment paper.
2. In a saucepan, combine the milk and vegetable oil.
3. Heat the mixture over medium heat until it starts to boil, then remove it from the heat.
4. In a large mixing bowl, add the tapioca flour and salt.
5. Pour the hot milk and oil mixture over the flour and stir well to combine.
6. Let the mixture cool for a few minutes until it is safe to handle, but still warm.
7. Beat the eggs in a separate bowl and then add them to the tapioca flour mixture.
8. Mix until the eggs are fully incorporated.
9. Add the grated cheese to the bowl and continue to mix until you have a smooth and sticky dough.
10. Using wet hands, shape the dough into small balls, about 1-2 inches in diameter. Place them on the prepared baking sheet, leaving some space between each ball.
11. Bake the pão de queijo in the preheated oven for about 20-25 minutes or until they turn golden brown.
12. Remove from the oven and let them cool for a few minutes before serving.

13. Enjoy the pão de queijo warm as a delightful snack or alongside your favorite meals.

Moqueca de Peixe

A flavorful fish stew made with coconut milk, tomatoes, peppers, and herbs, commonly served with rice.

Ingredients:

1.5 lbs white fish fillets (such as cod, snapper, or halibut), cut into chunks
1 onion, sliced
3 cloves of garlic, minced
1 red bell pepper, sliced
1 green bell pepper, sliced
1 can (14 oz) diced tomatoes
1 can (14 oz) coconut milk
2 tbsps. dendê oil (palm oil), optional but traditional
2 tbsps. lime juice
2 tbsps. fresh cilantro, chopped
2 tbsps. fresh parsley, chopped
Salt and pepper to taste

Directions:

1. In a large, deep skillet or pot, heat the dendê oil (if using) over medium heat.
2. Add the onion, garlic, and bell peppers. Sauté until they become softened and fragrant.
3. Add the diced tomatoes (with their juices) to the pot and stir to combine.
4. Let it simmer for a few minutes.
5. Pour in the coconut milk and bring the mixture to a gentle simmer.
6. Let it cook for about 10 minutes, allowing the flavors to meld together.
7. Season the fish chunks with salt and pepper, then add them to the pot. Gently stir to coat the fish with the sauce. Cover the pot and let the fish cook for about 5-8 minutes, or until it is cooked through and flakes easily.
8. Stir in the lime juice, fresh cilantro, and parsley. Adjust the seasoning with salt and pepper if needed.

9. Remove from heat and let the moqueca de peixe rest for a few minutes before serving.
10. Serve the moqueca de peixe hot with steamed rice and/or farofa (toasted cassava flour) on the side.

Brigadeiro

A popular Brazilian sweet treat made with condensed milk, cocoa powder, butter, and chocolate sprinkles.

Ingredients:

1 can (14 oz) sweetened condensed milk
2 tbsps. unsweetened cocoa powder
2 tbsps. butter
Chocolate sprinkles (or other desired toppings)

Directions:

1. In a medium-sized saucepan, combine the sweetened condensed milk, cocoa powder, and butter.
2. Place the saucepan over medium heat and cook the mixture, stirring continuously with a wooden spoon or spatula.
3. Keep stirring until the mixture thickens and starts to pull away from the sides of the pan. This process can take about 10-15 minutes.
4. Once the mixture has thickened and you can see the bottom of the pan as you stir, remove it from the heat.
5. Transfer the mixture to a greased plate or shallow dish and let it cool to room temperature.
6. Once the mixture is cool enough to handle, grease your hands with butter or oil to prevent sticking. Take small portions of the mixture and roll them into small balls, about 1-inch in diameter.
7. Roll the brigadeiros in chocolate sprinkles (or other desired toppings) until they are fully coated.
8. Place the brigadeiros in small paper cups or onto a plate lined with wax paper.
9. Repeat the process until all the mixture is used.
10. Let the brigadeiros set and cool completely before serving.

Acarajé

Deep-fried balls of black-eyed pea dough filled with shrimp, vatapá (spicy shrimp and peanut paste), and caruru (okra and shrimp sauce).

Acarajé Dough Ingredients:

2 cups dried black-eyed peas
1 small onion, finely chopped
2 cloves of garlic, minced
1 tbsp. ground dried shrimp (optional)
1 tsp. salt
Vegetable oil for frying
For the shrimp filling:
1 lb shrimp, peeled and deveined
2 cloves of garlic, minced
1 tbsp. lime juice
Salt and pepper to taste
For the toppings (optional):
Dried shrimp, ground
Vatapá (spicy shrimp and peanut paste)
Caruru (okra and shrimp sauce)
Sliced tomatoes
Thinly sliced onions
Hot sauce or chili paste

Directions:

1. Place the dried black-eyed peas in a bowl and cover them with water.
2. Let them soak overnight.
3. Drain the soaked black-eyed peas and transfer them to a food processor or blender.
4. Add the chopped onion, minced garlic, ground dried shrimp (if using), and salt. Blend until you have a thick and smooth batter.
5. In a deep pan or pot, heat vegetable oil for frying. The oil should be at least 2 inches deep.

6. Using a spoon or your hands, drop spoonfuls of the batter into the hot oil, shaping them into small round disks. Fry them in batches until they turn golden brown and crispy on both sides. Remove and drain on paper towels.
7. In a separate skillet, heat a little oil over medium heat.
8. Add the minced garlic and cook until fragrant.
9. Add the peeled shrimp, lime juice, salt, and pepper.
10. Cook until the shrimp are pink and cooked through. Remove from heat.
11. To assemble the acarajé, carefully split the fried dough disks in half horizontally, creating a pocket.
12. Fill the pocket with a spoonful of the cooked shrimp, and add desired toppings such as ground dried shrimp, vatapá, caruru, sliced tomatoes, onions, and hot sauce.
13. Serve the acarajé while still warm.

Caipirinha

Brazil's national cocktail made with cachaça (a sugarcane spirit), lime, sugar, and ice. It's a refreshing and tangy drink.

Ingredients:

2 oz. cachaça (Brazilian sugarcane liquor)
1 lime, cut into wedges
2 tbsps. granulated sugar
Crushed ice

Directions:

1. Place the lime wedges and sugar in a sturdy glass or cocktail shaker.
2. Muddle the lime and sugar together to release the lime juice and dissolve the sugar.
3. Add the cachaça to the glass or shaker and fill it with crushed ice.
4. Stir or shake well to mix all the ingredients together.
5. Pour the mixture, including the crushed ice, into a rocks glass.
6. Optionally, you can garnish with a lime wedge or slice.
7. Serve the Caipirinha immediately and enjoy!

Bobó de Camarão

A creamy shrimp stew made with yuca (cassava) purée, coconut milk, palm oil, tomatoes, and spices.

Ingredients:

1.5 lbs shrimp, peeled and deveined
1 lb yuca (cassava), peeled and cut into chunks
1 onion, finely chopped
3 cloves of garlic, minced
1 red bell pepper, diced
1 green bell pepper, diced
1 can (14 oz) coconut milk
2 tbsps. dendê oil (palm oil)
1 tbsp. tomato paste
1 tbsp. lime juice
2 tbsps. fresh cilantro, chopped
Salt and pepper to taste

Directions:

1. Place the yuca chunks in a large pot, cover with water, and bring to a boil.
2. Cook until the yuca is tender and easily pierced with a fork. Drain and set aside.
3. In a large skillet or pot, heat the dendê oil over medium heat.
4. Add the chopped onion, minced garlic, and diced bell peppers. Sauté until they become softened and fragrant.
5. Add the tomato paste to the skillet and cook for a minute, stirring well to incorporate it into the mixture.
6. Add the shrimp to the skillet and cook until they turn pink and opaque, stirring occasionally.
7. Transfer the cooked yuca to a blender or food processor.
8. Add the coconut milk and blend until you have a smooth and creamy mixture.
9. Pour the yuca and coconut milk mixture into the skillet with the cooked shrimp and vegetables.
10. Stir well to combine.

11. Simmer the mixture over low heat for about 10 minutes, allowing the flavors to meld together. Season with salt and pepper to taste.
12. Stir in the lime juice and fresh cilantro.
13. Remove from heat and let the Bobó de Camarão rest for a few minutes before serving.
14. Serve the Bobó de Camarão hot with steamed rice or with traditional accompaniments like farofa (toasted cassava flour) and vinaigrette salsa.

Quindim

A baked dessert made with egg yolks, sugar, coconut, and butter, resulting in a custard-like texture with a golden crust.

Ingredients:

10 egg yolks
1 and 1/4 cups sugar
1 cup unsweetened shredded coconut
1/4 cup melted butter
1/2 cup water
Butter or oil for greasing the molds
Additional shredded coconut for garnish (optional)

Directions:

1. Preheat your oven to 350°F (175°C).
2. In a large mixing bowl, combine the egg yolks, sugar, shredded coconut, melted butter, and water.
3. Stir well until all the ingredients are fully combined.
4. Grease individual custard cups or ramekins with butter or oil.
5. Pour the mixture into the greased molds, filling them about 2/3 of the way.
6. Place the molds in a baking dish and pour hot water into the dish, around halfway up the sides of the molds. This creates a water bath to gently cook the quindim.
7. Carefully transfer the baking dish to the preheated oven and bake for approximately 40-45 minutes, or until the quindim is set and the top is golden brown.
8. Remove the baking dish from the oven and let the quindim cool in the water bath.
9. Once the quindim has cooled, carefully remove them from the molds by running a knife around the edges and inverting them onto a serving plate.
10. If desired, garnish the quindim with additional shredded coconut.

11. Refrigerate the quindim for at least a couple of hours before serving to allow them to firm up and enhance their flavor.

Empadao de Frango

A chicken pot pie-like dish with a flaky crust.
Ingredients for the dough:

3 cups all-purpose flour
1 cup unsalted butter, cold and cubed
1 tsp. salt
1 egg yolk
4 tbsps. ice water
Filling Ingredients
2 tbsps. vegetable oil
1 onion, finely chopped
2 cloves of garlic, minced
2 cups cooked chicken, shredded or diced
1 carrot, finely chopped
1/2 cup frozen peas
1/2 cup corn kernels
1/2 cup chicken broth
1/2 cup heavy cream
2 tbsps. all-purpose flour
Salt and pepper to taste
1 egg, beaten (for egg wash)
Dough Instructions:
1. In a large mixing bowl, combine the flour and salt.
2. Add the cold, cubed butter to the flour mixture. Use a pastry cutter or your fingers to cut the butter into the flour until it resembles coarse crumbs.
3. In a small bowl, whisk together the egg yolk and ice water.
4. Gradually add the egg yolk mixture to the flour mixture, stirring with a fork, until the dough starts to come together.
5. Transfer the dough onto a lightly floured surface and knead it gently until it forms a smooth ball. Wrap the dough in plastic wrap and refrigerate for at least 30 minutes.

Filling Instructions:
1. In a large skillet, heat the vegetable oil over medium heat.
2. Add the chopped onion and minced garlic to the skillet and sauté until they become translucent and fragrant.
3. Add the cooked chicken, carrot, peas, and corn to the skillet.
4. Cook for a few minutes, stirring occasionally.
5. In a small bowl, whisk together the chicken broth, heavy cream, and flour until smooth.
6. Pour the broth mixture into the skillet with the chicken and vegetables.
7. Stir well to combine.
8. Cook the mixture over medium heat until it thickens and the vegetables are cooked through. Season with salt and pepper to taste. Remove from heat and let it cool.

Assembly Instructions:
1. Preheat your oven to 350°F (175°C).
2. Take the chilled dough out of the refrigerator and divide it into two equal portions (one slightly larger than the other).
3. On a lightly floured surface, roll out the larger portion of dough to fit the bottom and sides of a greased 9-inch pie dish or springform pan.
4. Carefully transfer the rolled dough to the pie dish, pressing it against the bottom and sides.
5. Pour the cooled chicken filling into the dish and spread it evenly.
6. Roll out the smaller portion of dough to cover the top of the pie. You can create a lattice pattern or simply cover it entirely with the dough. Press the edges to seal.
7. Brush the top of the pie with the beaten egg, which will give it a golden color.
8. Bake in the preheated oven for about 40-45 minutes, or until the crust is golden brown and the filling is bubbling.
9. Remove from the oven and let it cool for a few minutes before slicing and serving.

Vatapá

A spicy shrimp and peanut paste often used as a filling or topping.

Ingredients:

1 lb shrimp, peeled and deveined
4 slices of bread, crusts removed and soaked in water
1 cup unsweetened shredded coconut
1 onion, finely chopped
2 cloves of garlic, minced
2 tbsps. dendê oil (palm oil)
1 tbsp. ground dried shrimp (optional)
1 cup unsalted peanuts, ground or crushed
1 cup coconut milk
1 cup shrimp broth or water
1 tbsp. lime juice
1 tbsp. fresh cilantro, chopped
Salt and pepper to taste

Directions:

1. In a blender or food processor, blend the soaked bread and shredded coconut until you have a smooth paste. Set aside.
2. In a large skillet or pot, heat the dendê oil over medium heat.
3. Add the chopped onion and minced garlic, and sauté until they become translucent and fragrant.
4. Add the ground dried shrimp (if using) to the skillet and cook for a minute, stirring well to incorporate it into the mixture.
5. Add the ground peanuts to the skillet and cook for another minute, stirring constantly to prevent burning.
6. Stir in the coconut milk and shrimp broth (or water) into the skillet.
7. Mix well to combine.
8. Bring the mixture to a simmer and add the shrimp.

9. Cook for about 5-7 minutes until the shrimp are cooked through.
10. Gradually add the bread and coconut paste to the skillet, stirring continuously to avoid any lumps from forming.
11. Continue cooking over low heat, stirring constantly, until the mixture thickens to a creamy consistency. This should take about 10-15 minutes.
12. Season with salt, pepper, and lime juice to taste. Adjust the seasoning as desired.
13. Remove from heat and stir in the fresh cilantro.
14. Serve the Vatapá hot, accompanied by steamed rice or as a filling for acarajé (deep-fried black-eyed pea dough).
15. Garnish with additional cilantro, if desired.

Caruru

A flavorful okra and shrimp stew served as a side dish.

Ingredients:

1 lb okra, fresh or frozen
1 lb shrimp, peeled and deveined
1 onion, finely chopped
3 cloves of garlic, minced
2 tbsps. dendê oil (palm oil)
1 tbsp. ground dried shrimp (optional)
1 cup unsalted peanuts, ground or crushed
2 cups shrimp broth or water
1 cup coconut milk
1 tbsp. fresh cilantro, chopped
Salt and pepper to taste

Directions:

1. If using fresh okra, wash and trim the ends. Cut the okra into small pieces. If using frozen okra, thaw it according to package instructions.
2. In a large skillet or pot, heat the dendê oil over medium heat.
3. Add the chopped onion and minced garlic, and sauté until they become translucent and fragrant.
4. Add the ground dried shrimp (if using) to the skillet and cook for a minute, stirring well to incorporate it into the mixture.
5. Add the ground peanuts to the skillet and cook for another minute, stirring constantly to prevent burning.
6. Stir in the shrimp broth (or water) and coconut milk into the skillet.
7. Mix well to combine.
8. Bring the mixture to a simmer and add the shrimp and okra.
9. Cook for about 5-7 minutes until the shrimp are cooked through and the okra is tender.

10. Season with salt and pepper to taste. Adjust the seasoning as desired.
11. Remove from heat and stir in the fresh cilantro.
12. Serve the Caruru hot, accompanied by steamed rice and/or traditional Brazilian side dishes like farofa and acarajé.

Quibe

Ground meat (usually beef or lamb) mixed with bulgur wheat, onions, and spices, then baked or fried.

Ingredients:

1 1/2 cups fine bulgur wheat
1 lb ground beef or lamb
1 onion, finely chopped
3 cloves of garlic, minced
1/4 cup fresh mint leaves, finely chopped
1/4 cup fresh parsley, finely chopped
1 tsp. ground cumin
1 tsp. ground coriander
1/2 tsp. ground cinnamon
Salt and pepper to taste
Vegetable oil (for frying)

Optional filling Ingredients:

1/2 cup ground beef or lamb, cooked with spices and cooled (optional)

Directions:

1. Rinse the bulgur wheat under cold water, then place it in a bowl and cover it with water.
2. Let it soak for about 30 minutes until the wheat softens. Drain any excess water and set aside.
3. In a large mixing bowl, combine the ground beef or lamb, chopped onion, minced garlic, fresh mint, fresh parsley, cumin, coriander, cinnamon, salt, and pepper.
4. Add the soaked bulgur wheat to the meat mixture and mix well until all the ingredients are thoroughly combined.
5. The mixture should be moist but hold its shape.

6. If using the optional filling, take a small portion of the meat mixture, flatten it in your palm, and place a spoonful of the cooked ground meat filling in the center. Fold the edges over to enclose the filling and shape it into a torpedo-like or oval shape.
7. Repeat this process with the remaining mixture.
8. Heat vegetable oil in a deep skillet or fryer to a medium-high temperature (around 350°F or 180°C).
9. Carefully place the quibe in the hot oil and fry them in batches until they turn golden brown and crispy on the outside. This usually takes about 3-4 minutes per side.
10. Once cooked, transfer the fried quibe to a paper towel-lined plate to drain excess oil.
11. Serve the quibe hot as an appetizer or main dish. It pairs well with a side of yogurt or tzatziki sauce.

Escondidinho

A layered casserole dish typically made with mashed cassava or potatoes, meat (such as beef or shrimp), and cheese.

Meat Filling Ingredients:

1 lb ground beef or shredded chicken
1 onion, finely chopped
2 cloves of garlic, minced
1 tomato, diced
2 tbsps. vegetable oil
1 tsp. ground cumin
1 tsp. paprika
Salt and pepper to taste
1/4 cup fresh parsley, chopped
1/4 cup olives, sliced (optional)

Mashed Cassava/Potatoes Ingredients:

2 lbs cassava or potatoes, peeled and cut into chunks
4 tbsps. butter
1/2 cup milk
Salt to taste

Topping Ingredients:

1 cup grated cheese (cheddar or mozzarella)

Directions:

1. Preheat your oven to 375°F (190°C).
2. Prepare the meat filling: In a large skillet, heat the vegetable oil over medium heat.
3. Add the chopped onion and minced garlic, and sauté until they become translucent and fragrant.
4. Add the ground beef or shredded chicken to the skillet and cook until browned. If using ground beef, break it up into small pieces while cooking.
5. Add the diced tomato, ground cumin, paprika, salt, and pepper to the skillet.
6. Stir well to combine.

7. Cook for a few minutes until the tomato softens.
8. Add the chopped parsley and olives (if using) to the skillet and mix them into the meat filling. Remove from heat and set aside.
9. Prepare the mashed cassava or potatoes: Place the cassava or potato chunks in a large pot of salted water. Bring to a boil and cook until they are tender when pierced with a fork.
10. Drain the cooked cassava or potatoes and return them to the pot.
11. Add the butter and milk, and mash them together until smooth. Season with salt to taste.

Assembly Ingredients:

1. In a baking dish, spread half of the mashed cassava or potato mixture evenly to create a bottom layer.
2. Spoon the meat filling on top of the mashed cassava or potatoes, spreading it out evenly.
3. Add the remaining mashed cassava or potato mixture as the top layer, smoothing it out with a spatula.
4. Sprinkle the grated cheese evenly over the top of the dish.
5. Place the baking dish in the preheated oven and bake for about 25-30 minutes, or until the cheese is melted and bubbly.
6. Remove from the oven and let it cool for a few minutes before serving.
7. Serve the Escondidinho hot as a main dish, accompanied by a side salad.

Frango à Passarinho

Fried chicken pieces seasoned with garlic, herbs, and lime juice.

Ingredients:

1 lb chicken wings or drumettes, cut into small pieces
4 cloves of garlic, minced
Juice of 1 lemon
1 tsp. salt
1/2 tsp. black pepper
Vegetable oil (for frying)
Fresh parsley, chopped (for garnish)
Lime wedges (for serving)

Directions:

1. In a large bowl, combine the minced garlic, lemon juice, salt, and black pepper.
2. Add the chicken pieces to the bowl and toss them in the marinade until well coated.
3. Let it marinate for at least 30 minutes, or refrigerate overnight for enhanced flavor.
4. Heat vegetable oil in a deep skillet or deep fryer to medium-high heat.
5. Carefully add the marinated chicken pieces to the hot oil, making sure not to overcrowd the pan. Fry them in batches if necessary.
6. Fry the chicken pieces for about 8-10 minutes, turning occasionally, until they turn golden brown and crispy on the outside.
7. Use a slotted spoon or tongs to remove the fried chicken from the oil and transfer them to a paper towel-lined plate to drain excess oil.
8. Repeat the frying process with the remaining chicken pieces until all are cooked.
9. Once all the chicken pieces are fried, transfer them to a serving platter.

10. Garnish with fresh chopped parsley for added flavor and presentation.
11. Serve Frango à Passarinho hot, accompanied by lime wedges for squeezing over the chicken.

Salpicão

A festive chicken salad with a variety of vegetables, fruits, and a creamy dressing.

Ingredients:

2 cups cooked chicken breast, shredded or diced
1 cup carrots, grated
1 cup green apples, diced
1 cup canned pineapple, drained and diced
1/2 cup raisins
1/2 cup green peas, cooked and cooled
1/2 cup corn kernels, cooked and cooled
1/2 cup mayonnaise
1/4 cup sour cream
1 tbsp. Dijon mustard
1 tbsp. lemon juice
Salt and pepper to taste
Lettuce leaves (for serving)
Chopped fresh parsley (for garnish)

Directions:

1. In a large mixing bowl, combine the cooked chicken breast, grated carrots, diced green apples, diced pineapple, raisins, green peas, and corn kernels.
2. In a separate smaller bowl, whisk together the mayonnaise, sour cream, Dijon mustard, lemon juice, salt, and pepper until well combined.
3. Pour the dressing over the chicken and vegetable mixture. Toss gently until everything is well coated with the dressing.
4. Taste and adjust the seasoning, if needed, by adding more salt, pepper, or lemon juice.
5. Cover the bowl with plastic wrap and refrigerate for at least 30 minutes to allow the flavors to meld together.
6. Before serving, line a serving platter or individual plates with lettuce leaves.

7. Spoon the chilled Salpicão onto the lettuce leaves, forming a mound in the center.
8. Garnish with chopped fresh parsley for added freshness and presentation.
9. Serve the Salpicão chilled as a side dish or main course. It pairs well with bread, crackers, or as a topping for sandwiches.

Tutu de Feijão

A traditional dish made with mashed beans, sautéed onions, and spices.

Ingredients:

2 cups cooked black beans (or 1 can of black beans, drained and rinsed)
1 cup cassava flour (also known as farinha de mandioca or farofa)
4 slices of bacon, diced
1 onion, finely chopped
3 cloves of garlic, minced
2 tbsps. vegetable oil
1 tsp. ground cumin
Salt and pepper to taste
Fresh parsley, chopped (for garnish)

Directions:

1. In a large saucepan, heat the vegetable oil over medium heat.
2. Add the diced bacon and cook until crispy and the fat has rendered.
3. Remove about half of the cooked bacon from the pan and set it aside for garnishing the dish later.
4. Add the chopped onion to the saucepan and sauté until it becomes translucent and fragrant.
5. Add the minced garlic to the saucepan and sauté for an additional minute.
6. Add the cooked black beans to the saucepan and stir well to combine with the bacon, onion, and garlic mixture.
7. Using a potato masher or the back of a wooden spoon, partially mash the black beans to create a thick and creamy texture.
8. Gradually add the cassava flour to the saucepan, stirring continuously, until the mixture thickens.
9. Adjust the amount of cassava flour according to your desired consistency.

10. Season the tutu de feijão with ground cumin, salt, and pepper to taste.
11. Stir well to incorporate the seasonings.
12. Continue cooking the mixture for a few more minutes until it reaches a thick and smooth consistency.
13. Remove from heat and transfer the tutu de feijão to a serving dish.
14. Sprinkle the reserved crispy bacon over the top as a garnish.
15. Garnish with fresh chopped parsley for added freshness and presentation.
16. Serve the tutu de feijão hot as a side dish or as a main course, accompanied by white rice, sautéed collard greens, and your choice of protein.

Brigadeirão

A larger version of brigadeiro, a rich chocolate fudge-like dessert.

Ingredients:

4 tbsps. unsalted butter, melted
1 can (14 oz) sweetened condensed milk
4 tbsps. cocoa powder
4 large eggs
1 tsp. vanilla extract
Chocolate sprinkles (for garnish)

Directions:

1. Preheat your oven to 350°F (175°C). Grease a round cake pan or a fluted tube pan (Bundt pan) with butter or cooking spray.
2. In a blender or food processor, combine the melted butter, sweetened condensed milk, cocoa powder, eggs, and vanilla extract. Blend until all the ingredients are well combined and smooth.
3. Pour the mixture into the greased cake pan.
4. Place the cake pan in a larger baking dish or roasting pan. Fill the larger pan with hot water, creating a water bath (also known as a bain-marie) around the cake pan. The water should reach about halfway up the sides of the cake pan.
5. Carefully transfer the pans to the preheated oven and bake for approximately 50-60 minutes, or until the Brigadeirão is set in the center. The top may appear slightly cracked.
6. Remove the pans from the oven and let the Brigadeirão cool in the water bath for a few minutes.
7. Carefully remove the cake pan from the water bath and allow the Brigadeirão to cool completely at room temperature.

8. Once cooled, cover the cake pan with plastic wrap and refrigerate for at least 4 hours or overnight to allow it to firm up.
9. When ready to serve, remove the Brigadeirão from the refrigerator and carefully invert it onto a serving platter.
10. Gently tap the bottom of the pan if needed to release the dessert.
11. Garnish the top of the Brigadeirão with chocolate sprinkles, covering the surface.
12. Slice the Brigadeirão into wedges and serve chilled.
13. It can be enjoyed on its own or served with whipped cream, fresh berries, or ice cream.

Arroz de Carreteiro

A hearty rice dish with beef, onions, garlic, and spices.

Ingredients:

1 lb beef (such as flank steak or beef chuck), diced into small pieces
1 onion, finely chopped
2 cloves of garlic, minced
2 tbsps. vegetable oil
1 cup long-grain white rice
2 cups beef broth
1 tomato, diced
1 red bell pepper, diced
1 green bell pepper, diced
1 tsp. ground cumin
Salt and pepper to taste
Fresh parsley, chopped (for garnish)

Directions:

1. In a large skillet or Dutch oven, heat the vegetable oil over medium-high heat.
2. Add the diced beef to the skillet and cook until browned on all sides. Remove the beef from the skillet and set it aside.
3. In the same skillet, add the chopped onion and minced garlic. Sauté until the onion becomes translucent and fragrant.
4. Add the diced tomatoes and bell peppers to the skillet.
5. Cook for a few minutes until they soften slightly.
6. Return the browned beef to the skillet and stir well to combine with the vegetables.
7. Add the rice to the skillet and stir it into the mixture, ensuring it is evenly coated with the oil and flavors.
8. Pour the beef broth into the skillet and season with ground cumin, salt, and pepper to taste.
9. Stir well to combine.
10. Bring the mixture to a boil, then reduce the heat to low.

11. Cover the skillet with a lid and simmer for about 15-20 minutes, or until the rice is cooked and has absorbed the liquid.
12. Remove the skillet from the heat and let it rest, covered, for an additional 5 minutes.
13. Fluff the rice with a fork, mixing in the beef and vegetables evenly.
14. Garnish with fresh chopped parsley for added freshness and presentation.
15. Serve the Arroz de Carreteiro hot as a main dish, accompanied by a side of beans, salad, or vegetables.

Romeu e Julieta

A simple and delicious dessert pairing of guava paste and cheese.

Ingredients:

8 oz guava paste (also known as goiabada), cut into small cubes
8 oz cream cheese, softened
Crackers or plain butter cookies (for serving)

Directions:

1. Arrange the guava paste cubes and cream cheese on a serving platter or individual dessert plates.
2. Serve the guava paste and cream cheese together, allowing each person to create their own combinations.
3. Take a small piece of guava paste and spread a dollop of cream cheese on top.
4. Alternatively, you can sandwich a piece of guava paste between two slices of cream cheese.
5. Serve the Romeu e Julieta combinations with crackers or plain butter cookies on the side.
6. Guests can assemble their own Romeu e Julieta bites by spreading or layering the guava paste and cream cheese onto the crackers or cookies.
7. Enjoy the sweet and tangy flavor combination of Romeu e Julieta as a delightful dessert or snack.

Canjica

A sweet porridge made from boiled white corn, milk, coconut, and cinnamon.

Ingredients:

1 cup dried white corn kernels (canjica or hominy)
4 cups water
1 can (14 oz) sweetened condensed milk
1 can (13.5 oz) coconut milk
1 cup whole milk
1/2 cup granulated sugar
1 cinnamon stick
Ground cinnamon (for garnish)

Directions:

1. Rinse the dried white corn kernels thoroughly under running water to remove any impurities.
2. In a large pot, combine the rinsed corn kernels and water. Bring to a boil over medium heat.
3. Reduce the heat to low, cover the pot, and simmer for about 1 to 1 1/2 hours, or until the corn kernels are soft and cooked through.
4. Stir occasionally and add more water if necessary to prevent sticking or burning.
5. Once the corn kernels are tender, drain any excess water from the pot.
6. Add the sweetened condensed milk, coconut milk, whole milk, granulated sugar, and cinnamon stick to the pot with the cooked corn kernels.
7. Stir well to combine all the ingredients and bring the mixture to a gentle simmer over low heat.
8. Cook the canjica, uncovered, for about 20-30 minutes, stirring occasionally, until the mixture thickens and reaches a creamy consistency.
9. Remove the cinnamon stick from the pot and discard it.
10. Transfer the canjica to serving bowls or a large serving dish.

11. Sprinkle ground cinnamon on top of the canjica for added flavor and garnish.

Pudim de Leite Condensado

A creamy and caramel-topped condensed milk flan.

Caramel Ingredients:

1 cup granulated sugar
1/4 cup water

Pudding Ingredients:

4 eggs
1 can (14 oz) sweetened condensed milk
1 cup whole milk
1 tsp. vanilla extract

Directions:

1. Preheat your oven to 350°F (175°C).
2. In a small saucepan, combine the granulated sugar and water for the caramel.
3. Heat over medium-high heat, stirring occasionally until the sugar dissolves and the mixture turns amber in color.
4. Immediately pour the caramel into a 9-inch round cake pan, swirling the pan to evenly distribute the caramel along the bottom and slightly up the sides. Be careful as the caramel will be extremely hot. Set the pan aside to allow the caramel to cool and harden.
5. In a blender or mixing bowl, combine the eggs, sweetened condensed milk, whole milk, and vanilla extract. Blend or whisk until smooth and well combined.
6. Pour the pudding mixture into the prepared cake pan with the hardened caramel.
7. Place the cake pan inside a larger baking dish or roasting pan. Fill the larger pan with hot water, creating a water bath (bain-marie) around the cake pan. The water should reach about halfway up the sides of the cake pan.
8. Carefully transfer the pans to the preheated oven and bake for approximately 50-60 minutes, or until the pudding is set and a toothpick inserted into the center comes out clean.

9. Remove the pans from the oven and carefully remove the cake pan from the water bath. Allow the pudding to cool to room temperature.
10. Once cooled, cover the cake pan with plastic wrap and refrigerate for at least 4 hours or overnight to allow the pudding to firm up and fully set.
11. To serve, run a knife around the edges of the pan to loosen the pudding. Place a serving plate upside down on top of the pan, then carefully flip the pan and plate together, releasing the pudding onto the plate.
12. The caramel will drizzle down the sides of the pudding, creating a delicious topping.
13. Slice and serve the Pudim de Leite Condensado chilled.

Bolo de Fubá

A moist cornmeal cake often flavored with cheese or coconut.

Ingredients:

1 ½ cups fine cornmeal (fubá)
1 cup all-purpose flour
1 ½ cups granulated sugar
3 tbsps. unsalted butter, softened
3 eggs
1 cup milk
1 tbsp. baking powder
1 tsp. vanilla extract
Pinch of salt

Directions:

1. Preheat your oven to 350°F (175°C). Grease and flour a round cake pan or line it with parchment paper.
2. In a large bowl, cream together the softened butter and sugar until light and fluffy.
3. Add the eggs one at a time, beating well after each addition.
4. Stir in the vanilla extract.
5. In a separate bowl, whisk together the cornmeal, flour, baking powder, and salt.
6. Gradually add the dry ingredients to the butter mixture, alternating with the milk. Begin and end with the dry ingredients, mixing well after each addition.
7. Pour the batter into the prepared cake pan, smoothing the top with a spatula.
8. Bake in the preheated oven for about 35-40 minutes, or until a toothpick inserted into the center comes out clean.
9. Remove the cake from the oven and let it cool in the pan for a few minutes.
10. Transfer the cake to a wire rack to cool completely before serving.

11. Once cooled, slice and serve the Bolo de Fubá as a delightful accompaniment to coffee or tea, or enjoy it as a tasty snack on its own.

Cocada

A sweet treat made with shredded coconut, sugar, and often flavored with spices or fruits.

Ingredients:

2 cups grated coconut (fresh or desiccated)
1 ½ cups granulated sugar
½ cup water
1 tbsp. unsalted butter
1 tsp. vanilla extract
Pinch of salt

Directions:

1. In a medium-sized saucepan, combine the sugar, water, butter, vanilla extract, and salt.
2. Stir well to combine.
3. Place the saucepan over medium heat and bring the mixture to a boil, stirring constantly to dissolve the sugar.
4. Once the mixture comes to a boil, reduce the heat to low and add the grated coconut.
5. Stir the coconut into the syrup mixture, ensuring it is well coated.
6. Continue to cook the mixture over low heat, stirring frequently to prevent sticking or burning, for about 15-20 minutes or until the mixture thickens and the coconut becomes glossy.
7. Remove the saucepan from the heat and let the cocada cool for a few minutes.
8. Using a spoon or your hands, drop spoonfuls or shape the cocada into small mounds onto a greased baking sheet or parchment paper. Alternatively, you can pour the mixture into a greased square baking dish and let it cool before cutting into squares.
9. Allow the cocada to cool completely and firm up at room temperature.

10. Once cooled and firm, the cocada is ready to be enjoyed. You can store it in an airtight container at room temperature for several days.

Arroz de Camarão

A flavorful shrimp rice dish cooked with onions, garlic, tomatoes, and spices.

Ingredients:

1 lb shrimp, peeled and deveined
2 cups long-grain white rice
4 cups chicken or vegetable broth
1 onion, finely chopped
2 cloves of garlic, minced
1 bell pepper, diced
1 tomato, diced
2 tbsps. tomato paste
2 tbsps. olive oil
1 tsp. paprika
1/2 tsp. turmeric
1/2 tsp. dried oregano
Salt and pepper to taste
Fresh parsley or cilantro, chopped (for garnish)

Directions:

1. Rinse the rice under cold water until the water runs clear. Drain and set aside.
2. In a large skillet or Dutch oven, heat the olive oil over medium heat.
3. Add the chopped onion, minced garlic, and diced bell pepper to the skillet. Sauté until the vegetables are softened and aromatic.
4. Add the diced tomato and cook for a few minutes until it starts to break down.
5. Stir in the tomato paste, paprika, turmeric, dried oregano, salt, and pepper.
6. Cook for another minute to let the flavors meld together.
7. Add the shrimp to the skillet and cook until they turn pink and opaque, about 2-3 minutes per side. Remove the shrimp from the skillet and set aside.

8. In the same skillet, add the rice and stir to coat it with the flavorful mixture.
9. Cook for a couple of minutes to lightly toast the rice.
10. Pour the broth into the skillet and bring the mixture to a boil. Reduce the heat to low, cover the skillet with a lid, and simmer for about 15-20 minutes, or until the rice is cooked and has absorbed the liquid.
11. Once the rice is cooked, gently stir in the cooked shrimp, ensuring they are distributed evenly throughout the rice.
12. Cover the skillet and let it sit for a few minutes to allow the flavors to meld together.
13. Remove the lid and fluff the rice with a fork. Adjust the seasoning if needed.
14. Garnish with freshly chopped parsley or cilantro before serving.

Escondidinho de Carne Seca

A casserole made with dried and shredded beef, mashed cassava or potatoes, and cheese.

Filling Ingredients:

1 lb dried beef (carne seca)
2 tbsps. vegetable oil
1 onion, finely chopped
3 cloves of garlic, minced
1 bell pepper, diced
1 tomato, diced
1 tsp. ground cumin
1 tsp. paprika
Salt and pepper to taste
Water (for boiling the beef)

mashed cassava topping Ingredients:

2 lbs cassava (yuca), peeled and cut into chunks
4 tbsps. butter
1 cup milk
Salt to taste

Assembly Ingredients:

Shredded cheese (such as mozzarella or cheddar)

Directions:

1. Start by preparing the dried beef. Rinse it under cold water to remove excess salt. Place it in a large pot, cover it with water, and bring to a boil. Simmer for about 30 minutes to remove additional salt. Drain the beef and shred it into small pieces. Set aside.
2. In a large skillet, heat the vegetable oil over medium heat.
3. Add the chopped onion and minced garlic. Sauté until the onion is translucent and the garlic is fragrant.
4. Add the diced bell pepper and tomato to the skillet.
5. Cook for a few minutes until the vegetables soften.

6. Stir in the shredded beef, ground cumin, paprika, salt, and pepper.
7. Cook for another 5 minutes to allow the flavors to meld together. Adjust the seasoning if needed. Remove from heat and set aside.
8. Meanwhile, prepare the mashed cassava. Place the cassava chunks in a large pot and cover them with water. Bring to a boil and cook until the cassava is tender and easily pierced with a fork, about 20-25 minutes.
9. Drain the cassava and transfer it to a large mixing bowl.
10. Add the butter and milk. Mash the cassava until smooth and creamy. Season with salt to taste.
11. Preheat your oven to 350°F (175°C).
12. In a baking dish, spread half of the mashed cassava mixture to form the bottom layer.
13. Spread the prepared beef filling evenly over the cassava layer.
14. Sprinkle a generous amount of shredded cheese over the beef filling.
15. Top with the remaining mashed cassava, spreading it to cover the filling completely.
16. Sprinkle more shredded cheese on top as desired.
17. Place the baking dish in the preheated oven and bake for about 25-30 minutes, or until the cheese is melted and golden.
18. Remove from the oven and let it cool slightly before serving.

Baião de Dois

A traditional dish from the Northeast region, made with rice, black-eyed peas, dried beef, sausage, and spices.

Ingredients:

1 cup rice
1 cup black-eyed peas or cowpeas (previously soaked overnight)
4 slices of bacon, chopped
1 onion, finely chopped
2 cloves of garlic, minced
1 green bell pepper, diced
1 tomato, diced
2 tbsps. vegetable oil
1 tsp. ground cumin
1 tsp. paprika
Salt and pepper to taste
Fresh cilantro or parsley, chopped (for garnish)

Directions:

1. In a large pot, bring water to a boil and cook the soaked black-eyed peas until tender. Drain and set aside.
2. In a separate pot, cook the rice according to the package instructions. Once cooked, set it aside.
3. In a large skillet, heat the vegetable oil over medium heat.
4. Add the chopped bacon and cook until it becomes crispy.
5. Add the chopped onion, minced garlic, and diced bell pepper to the skillet. Sauté until the vegetables are softened and aromatic.
6. Stir in the diced tomato, ground cumin, paprika, salt, and pepper.
7. Cook for a few minutes until the tomato starts to break down.
8. Add the cooked black-eyed peas to the skillet and mix well with the seasoned vegetables.
9. Finally, add the cooked rice to the skillet and stir to combine all the ingredients.

10. Cook for a few minutes to allow the flavors to meld together.
11. Adjust the seasoning if needed.
12. Remove the skillet from the heat and garnish with fresh chopped cilantro or parsley.
13. Serve the Baião de Dois hot as a main course or as a side dish to complement other Brazilian dishes.

Beijinho de Coco

Coconut truffles made with condensed milk, butter, and rolled in coconut flakes.

Ingredients:

1 can (14 oz) sweetened condensed milk
1 tbsp. unsalted butter
1 cup shredded coconut (unsweetened or sweetened)
Cloves or whole cloves (for decoration)

Directions:

1. In a non-stick pan or skillet, combine the sweetened condensed milk, butter, and shredded coconut.
2. Cook the mixture over medium heat, stirring constantly to prevent sticking, for about 10-15 minutes or until it thickens and starts to pull away from the sides of the pan.
3. Remove the pan from the heat and let the mixture cool for a few minutes until it is safe to handle.
4. Grease your hands with a little butter to prevent sticking, then take small portions of the mixture and roll them into small balls, about 1 inch in diameter.
5. Place the Beijinhos de Coco on a baking sheet lined with parchment paper.
6. If desired, insert a clove or whole clove into the center of each beijinho for decoration.
7. Repeat the process until all the mixture is used.
8. Let the beijinhos cool completely at room temperature.
9. Once cooled, you can serve the Beijinhos de Coco immediately or store them in an airtight container in the refrigerator until ready to serve.
10. Enjoy these sweet and coconutty treats as a delightful dessert or as a special addition to a party or gathering!

Rabanada

Brazilian-style French toast, usually enjoyed during Christmas time, soaked in sweetened milk, coated in cinnamon sugar, and fried.

Ingredients:

1 loaf of day-old French bread or baguette, sliced into thick slices
2 cups milk
4 eggs
1/2 cup granulated sugar
1 tsp. ground cinnamon
Vegetable oil, for frying
Powdered sugar, for dusting

Directions:

1. In a shallow bowl, whisk together the milk and eggs until well combined.
2. In a separate bowl, mix the granulated sugar and ground cinnamon.
3. Heat vegetable oil in a large frying pan or skillet over medium heat.
4. Dip each bread slice into the milk and egg mixture, allowing it to soak for a few seconds on each side.
5. Carefully transfer the soaked bread slice to the hot oil and fry until golden brown on each side, about 2-3 minutes per side.
6. Remove the fried bread slices from the oil and drain on paper towels to remove excess oil.
7. While still warm, roll each slice in the sugar and cinnamon mixture until coated on all sides.
8. Place the coated Rabanadas on a serving platter and sprinkle with powdered sugar.
9. Serve the Rabanadas warm and enjoy them as a sweet breakfast or dessert.

Feijão Tropeiro

A hearty dish made with beans, collard greens, dried meat, sausage, and cassava flour.

Ingredients:

2 cups cooked black beans
1 cup manioc flour (also known as farofa)
4 slices of bacon, chopped
1/2 lb smoked sausage, sliced
1 onion, finely chopped
3 cloves of garlic, minced
2 hard-boiled eggs, chopped
Salt and pepper to taste
Chopped green onions or parsley (for garnish)

Directions:

1. In a large skillet or frying pan, cook the bacon over medium heat until it becomes crispy. Remove the bacon from the pan and set it aside, leaving the rendered fat in the pan.
2. In the same skillet, add the chopped onion and minced garlic. Sauté until the onion is translucent and the garlic is fragrant.
3. Add the sliced smoked sausage to the skillet and cook until it is browned and cooked through.
4. Stir in the cooked black beans and mix well with the sausage and onion mixture.
5. Gradually add the manioc flour to the skillet, stirring constantly to combine it with the other ingredients.
6. Cook for a few minutes to allow the flavors to meld together and for the farofa to absorb the flavors.
7. Season with salt and pepper to taste.
8. Remove the skillet from the heat and stir in the chopped hard-boiled eggs and reserved crispy bacon.
9. Transfer the Feijão Tropeiro to a serving dish and garnish with chopped green onions or parsley.

10. Serve the Feijão Tropeiro as a main dish or as a side dish alongside rice, meat, or other Brazilian dishes.

Bolo de Milho

A moist corn cake made with fresh corn, cornmeal, sugar, eggs, and coconut milk.

Ingredients:

1 can (14 oz) sweetened condensed milk
1 can (12 oz) corn kernels, drained
3 eggs
1/2 cup cornmeal
1/2 cup all-purpose flour
1/4 cup vegetable oil
1 tbsp. baking powder
1/2 tsp. salt
1/2 cup grated cheese (optional, for topping)

Directions:

1. Preheat your oven to 350°F (175°C). Grease and flour a cake pan.
2. In a blender or food processor, combine the sweetened condensed milk, corn kernels, eggs, and vegetable oil. Blend until smooth and well combined.
3. In a separate bowl, whisk together the cornmeal, all-purpose flour, baking powder, and salt.
4. Pour the wet mixture from the blender into the dry mixture and stir until everything is well combined.
5. Pour the batter into the prepared cake pan.
6. If desired, sprinkle grated cheese over the top of the batter for added flavor.
7. Bake in the preheated oven for approximately 30-35 minutes, or until a toothpick inserted into the center comes out clean.
8. Remove from the oven and let the Bolo de Milho cool in the pan for a few minutes.
9. Once cooled, transfer the cake to a serving plate.
10. Slice and serve the Bolo de Milho at room temperature.

Quibebe

A sweet pumpkin or winter squash puree flavored with spices, often served as a side dish.
ngredients:

1 butternut squash (approximately 2 lbs), peeled, seeded, and diced
1 onion, finely chopped
2 cloves of garlic, minced
2 tbsps. vegetable oil
Salt and pepper to taste
Chopped parsley or cilantro (for garnish)

Directions:

1. In a large pot, heat the vegetable oil over medium heat.
2. Add the chopped onion and minced garlic to the pot. Sauté until the onion is translucent and the garlic is fragrant.
3. Add the diced butternut squash to the pot and stir to combine with the onion and garlic mixture.
4. Reduce the heat to low, cover the pot, and let the squash cook for about 15-20 minutes, or until it becomes tender.
5. Stir occasionally to prevent sticking and ensure even cooking.
6. Once the squash is tender, use a potato masher or fork to mash the squash until it reaches a smooth consistency. Alternatively, you can use an immersion blender for a smoother texture.
7. Season the quibebe with salt and pepper to taste. Adjust the seasoning if needed.
8. Cook for another 5 minutes, stirring occasionally to incorporate the seasoning.
9. Remove the pot from the heat and transfer the quibebe to a serving dish.
10. Garnish with chopped parsley or cilantro.

11. Serve the Quibebe warm as a side dish to accompany meat, rice, or other Brazilian dishes.

Salpicao de Frango

Brazilian Chicken Salad

Ingredients:

1 pound coarsely shredded cooked chicken
1 (8 oz.) can whole kernel corn, drained
1 cup pitted green olives, chopped
¾ cup golden raisins
2 carrots, grated
1 stalk celery, finely chopped
¼ green apple, finely chopped
4 tbsps. heavy cream
1 tbsp. Dijon mustard
1 pinch white sugar
salt and freshly ground black pepper to taste
2 tbsps. chopped fresh parsley, or to taste
Garnish (optional):
2 large lettuce leaves
4 sprigs watercress
2 cups shoestring potato sticks

Directions:

1. Combine chicken, corn, olives, raisins, carrots, celery, and apple in a large bowl.
2. Stir together cream and mustard in a cup and season with sugar, salt, and pepper.
3. Pour dressing over salad and mix to combine. Season with salt and pepper and sprinkle with parsley.
4. Arrange lettuce leaves and watercress on a platter and spoon salad in the middle. Sprinkle shoestring potato sticks on top and press into salad. Chill until serving.

Bolo de Leite Condensado

Brazilian Condensed Milk Cake

Ingredients:

1 (14 oz.) can sweetened condensed milk
14 fluid oz. milk
2 eggs
2 tbsps. unsalted butter
2 cups all-purpose flour
1 cup white sugar
1 tbsp. baking powder
1 pinch salt

Directions:

1. Preheat oven to 350 degrees F (175 degrees C).
2. Grease and flour a 9-inch tube pan.
3. Place condensed milk, milk, eggs, and butter in a blender; blend until well-combined.
4. Add flour, sugar, baking powder, and salt; blend until cake batter is smooth.
5. Pour into prepared cake pan.
6. Bake in the preheated oven until golden brown, about 40 minutes.

Pastel

Crispy deep-fried pastries filled with various savory fillings like cheese, meat, or shrimp.

Ingredients:

2 cups all-purpose flour
1/2 tsp. salt
1/2 cup cold water
2 tbsps. vegetable oil
Fillings of your choice (e.g., ground meat, cheese, ham, chicken, vegetables)
Vegetable oil, for frying

Directions:

1. In a large mixing bowl, combine the all-purpose flour and salt.
2. Mix well.
3. Gradually add the cold water and vegetable oil to the flour mixture.
4. Stir until the dough starts to come together.
5. Transfer the dough to a clean surface and knead it for about 5 minutes until smooth and elastic. If the dough is too sticky, add a little more flour; if it's too dry, add a little more water.
6. Cover the dough with a clean kitchen towel and let it rest for about 30 minutes.
7. While the dough is resting, prepare the fillings of your choice. You can sauté ground meat with onions and spices, or mix grated cheese with ham or chicken, or use cooked vegetables seasoned to your liking.
8. After the resting time, divide the dough into small portions and roll each portion into a thin circle or rectangle. The size can vary depending on your preference.
9. Place a spoonful of your chosen filling in the center of each rolled dough portion.

10. Fold the dough over the filling to form a half-moon shape. Press the edges together to seal the pastel.
11. Repeat the process with the remaining dough and filling until you have used them all.
12. In a deep skillet or pot, heat vegetable oil over medium heat for frying.
13. Carefully add the pastels to the hot oil, a few at a time, and fry them until golden brown on both sides. This usually takes about 2-3 minutes per side.
14. Use a slotted spoon or tongs to remove the fried pastels from the oil and transfer them to a paper towel-lined plate to drain excess oil.
15. Serve the pastels hot and enjoy them as a delicious snack or appetizer.

Salgadinho de Queijo

Cheese balls made with cheese, flour, and butter, baked until golden and crispy.

Ingredients:

2 cups tapioca flour (also known as tapioca starch)
1 1/2 cups grated cheese (such as Parmesan, Cheddar, or a mix)
1/2 cup milk
1/4 cup vegetable oil
2 eggs
1 tsp. salt
Additional grated cheese for sprinkling (optional)

Directions:

1. Preheat your oven to 350°F (175°C). Line a baking sheet with parchment paper.
2. In a large mixing bowl, combine the tapioca flour, grated cheese, and salt.
3. Mix well to ensure the cheese is evenly distributed.
4. In a small saucepan, heat the milk and vegetable oil over medium heat until it starts to simmer. Remove from heat.
5. Pour the hot milk and oil mixture over the tapioca flour and cheese mixture.
6. Stir with a spoon or spatula until the mixture comes together and forms a dough-like consistency.
7. Allow the mixture to cool slightly, then add the eggs one at a time, mixing well after each addition. The dough should become smoother and more elastic.
8. Take small portions of the dough and roll them into small balls, about 1 inch in diameter. Place the balls on the prepared baking sheet, spacing them a few inches apart.
9. If desired, sprinkle some additional grated cheese on top of each ball for added flavor.
10. Bake the Salgadinhos de Queijo in the preheated oven for about 15-20 minutes, or until they are lightly golden and firm to the touch.

11. Remove the baking sheet from the oven and let the Salgadinhos cool for a few minutes before serving.

Moqueca de Camarão

A version of moqueca made specifically with shrimp as the main ingredient.

Ingredients:

1 lb (450g) shrimp, peeled and deveined
1 onion, sliced
1 red bell pepper, sliced
1 green bell pepper, sliced
2 tomatoes, diced
3 cloves of garlic, minced
1 tbsp. tomato paste
1 cup coconut milk
1 cup fish or vegetable broth
2 tbsps. lime juice
2 tbsps. fresh cilantro, chopped
2 tbsps. olive oil
Salt and pepper to taste

Directions:

1. In a large pot or deep skillet, heat the olive oil over medium heat.
2. Add the sliced onions, bell peppers, and minced garlic to the pot. Sauté until the vegetables are softened and slightly caramelized.
3. Stir in the diced tomatoes and tomato paste.
4. Cook for a few minutes until the tomatoes start to break down and release their juices.
5. Add the coconut milk and fish or vegetable broth to the pot.
6. Stir well to combine all the ingredients.
7. Bring the mixture to a simmer and let it cook for about 10 minutes, allowing the flavors to meld together.
8. Season the shrimp with salt, pepper, and lime juice.
9. Add the seasoned shrimp to the pot.
10. Gently stir the shrimp into the stew, ensuring they are fully submerged in the liquid.

11. Cook for approximately 5-7 minutes, or until the shrimp turn pink and are cooked through. Be careful not to overcook the shrimp, as they can become rubbery.
12. Sprinkle fresh cilantro over the top of the stew and give it a final stir.
13. Taste and adjust the seasoning if needed.
14. Remove the pot from the heat and let the Moqueca de Camarão rest for a few minutes.
15. Serve the Moqueca de Camarão hot with steamed rice and/or farofa (toasted manioc flour) on the side.

Brazilian Broa (Corn Bread)

Ingredients:

1 ½ cups white sugar
1 cup cornmeal
1 cup all-purpose flour
½ tsp. salt
2 eggs
1 cup milk, at room temperature
¼ cup melted butter

Directions:

1. Mix sugar, cornmeal, flour, and salt together in bowl until combined; add eggs.
2. Stir milk and melted butter in a bowl until smooth; stir into the cornmeal mixture until smooth, about 5 minutes.
3. Grease a griddle; place over high heat. Drop tablespoonfuls of the cornmeal mixture into the skillet; cook until golden brown, about 5 minutes each side.

Torta de Frango

A classic Brazilian chicken pie made with a flaky crust and a creamy chicken filling.

Dough Ingredients:

2 cups all-purpose flour
1/2 tsp. salt
1/2 cup unsalted butter, cold and diced
1/4 cup cold water

Filling Ingredients:

2 cups cooked chicken breast, shredded
1 onion, finely chopped
2 cloves of garlic, minced
1 carrot, diced
1/2 cup green peas
1/2 cup corn kernels
1/2 cup cream cheese
1/2 cup chicken broth
1 tbsp. olive oil
1 tsp. dried oregano
Salt and pepper to taste
1 egg, beaten (for egg wash)

Directions:

1. Preheat your oven to 375°F (190°C). Grease a pie dish or tart pan.
2. In a large mixing bowl, combine the flour and salt.
3. Add the diced cold butter and use your fingertips or a pastry cutter to rub the butter into the flour until the mixture resembles coarse crumbs.
4. Gradually add the cold water, a little at a time, and mix until the dough comes together. Form the dough into a ball and refrigerate for 30 minutes.
5. In a large skillet, heat the olive oil over medium heat.
6. Add the chopped onion and minced garlic, and sauté until the onion becomes translucent and the garlic is fragrant.

7. Add the diced carrot, green peas, and corn kernels to the skillet.
8. Cook for a few minutes until the vegetables start to soften.
9. Stir in the shredded chicken, dried oregano, salt, and pepper.
10. Cook for another few minutes to allow the flavors to meld together.
11. Pour in the chicken broth and bring the mixture to a simmer.
12. Cook for a few minutes until the liquid has reduced slightly.
13. Remove the skillet from the heat and stir in the cream cheese until it is well incorporated and forms a creamy filling. Adjust the seasoning if needed.
14. Take the dough out of the refrigerator and divide it into two portions - one slightly larger than the other.
15. Roll out the larger portion of dough on a floured surface until it is large enough to cover the bottom and sides of the pie dish.
16. Carefully transfer the rolled-out dough to the greased pie dish, pressing it gently to line the bottom and sides.
17. Pour the chicken filling into the prepared crust, spreading it evenly.
18. Roll out the smaller portion of dough to create a lid for the pie. Place it over the filling, pressing the edges to seal it with the bottom crust. You can crimp the edges or use a fork to create a decorative pattern.
19. Brush the beaten egg over the top of the pie, which will give it a golden color when baked.
20. Cut a few slits on the top crust to allow steam to escape during baking.
21. Bake the Torta de Frango in the preheated oven for about 30-35 minutes, or until the crust is golden brown and the filling is heated through.
22. Remove from the oven and let the pie cool for a few minutes before serving.
23. Slice and serve the Torta de Frango warm as a main course or as a delicious savory snack.

Manjar de Coco

A coconut pudding topped with a sweet fruit sauce, usually made from red berries or tropical fruits.

Ingredients:

1 cup coconut milk
2 cups whole milk
1 cup granulated sugar
1/2 cup cornstarch
1/2 cup shredded coconut (unsweetened)
1 tsp. vanilla extract
Caramel sauce (for serving, optional)
Shredded coconut (for garnish, optional)

Directions:

1. In a saucepan, combine the coconut milk, whole milk, and granulated sugar.
2. Stir well to dissolve the sugar.
3. Place the saucepan over medium heat and bring the mixture to a simmer, stirring occasionally to prevent the milk from scorching.
4. In a small bowl, whisk together the cornstarch and a few tbsps. of water to make a slurry. Make sure there are no lumps.
5. Slowly pour the cornstarch slurry into the simmering milk mixture while continuously whisking. This will help thicken the pudding.
6. Reduce the heat to low and continue whisking the mixture for about 5-7 minutes, or until it thickens to a custard-like consistency. The pudding should coat the back of a spoon.
7. Remove the saucepan from the heat and stir in the shredded coconut and vanilla extract.
8. Mix well.
9. Lightly grease a mold or individual ramekins with cooking spray or oil.

10. Pour the pudding mixture into the greased mold(s) and let it cool at room temperature for a few minutes.
11. Once cooled, cover the mold(s) with plastic wrap and refrigerate for at least 4 hours, or until set and chilled.
12. When ready to serve, carefully invert the mold(s) onto a serving platter to release the pudding. If using individual ramekins, you can serve them directly in the ramekins.
13. If desired, drizzle caramel sauce over the top of the manjar de coco and sprinkle some shredded coconut as a garnish.
14. Slice and serve the Manjar de Coco chilled as a delightful and creamy coconut dessert.

Cuscuz Paulista

A savory molded dish made with cornmeal, vegetables, and various fillings such as chicken, shrimp, or sardines.

Ingredients:

2 cups cornmeal (finely ground)
2 cups water
1/2 cup vegetable oil
1 onion, finely chopped
2 cloves of garlic, minced
1 red bell pepper, finely chopped
1 green bell pepper, finely chopped
1 carrot, grated
1 cup cooked ham, diced
1 cup cooked corn kernels
1 cup green peas (fresh or frozen)
1/2 cup pitted olives, sliced
1/4 cup chopped parsley
Salt and pepper to taste

Directions:

1. In a large bowl, combine the cornmeal and water.
2. Mix well until the cornmeal absorbs the water.
3. Let it sit for about 10 minutes to hydrate.
4. In a large skillet, heat the vegetable oil over medium heat.
5. Add the chopped onion and minced garlic, and sauté until the onion becomes translucent and the garlic is fragrant.
6. Add the chopped red and green bell peppers to the skillet. Sauté for a few minutes until the peppers start to soften.
7. Stir in the grated carrot, diced ham, cooked corn kernels, and green peas.
8. Cook for another few minutes until the vegetables are tender.
9. Season the mixture with salt and pepper according to your taste. Remember that the ham and olives will add some saltiness to the dish, so go easy on the salt if desired.

10. Add the sliced olives and chopped parsley to the skillet.
11. Mix well to distribute the ingredients evenly.
12. Carefully transfer the mixture from the skillet into the bowl with the hydrated cornmeal.
13. Mix everything together until well combined.
14. Lightly grease a round or rectangular mold with vegetable oil. Press the cornmeal mixture firmly into the mold, ensuring it is evenly distributed.
15. Cover the mold with aluminum foil and place it in a steamer or a large pot with a steamer basket. Fill the pot with water, making sure it doesn't touch the mold.
16. Steam the cuscuz over medium heat for about 45 minutes to 1 hour, or until it is firm and cooked through.
17. Remove the mold from the steamer and let it cool for a few minutes.
18. To serve, carefully invert the mold onto a serving platter to release the cuscuz. It should come out easily.
19. Slice the cuscuz into portions and serve it warm or at room temperature.

Rosca de Polvilho

A gluten-free cheese bread made with cassava starch and cheese, often enjoyed for breakfast or as a snack.

Ingredients:

4 cups tapioca starch
1 cup milk
1 cup vegetable oil
1 tsp. salt
4 eggs
1 cup grated Parmesan cheese (optional)
Additional tapioca starch for shaping

Directions:

1. Preheat your oven to 350°F (175°C). Line a baking sheet with parchment paper.
2. In a saucepan, heat the milk, vegetable oil, and salt over medium heat until it starts to simmer. Remove from heat.
3. In a large mixing bowl, add the tapioca starch.
4. Slowly pour the hot milk mixture into the tapioca starch while stirring with a wooden spoon.
5. Mix well until the dough comes together and forms a smooth and slightly sticky consistency.
6. Allow the dough to cool for a few minutes until it is comfortable to handle.
7. Beat the eggs in a separate bowl and gradually add them to the dough.
8. Mix well until the eggs are fully incorporated.
9. If desired, add the grated Parmesan cheese to the dough and mix until evenly distributed. This step is optional but adds extra flavor to the rosca.
10. Dust your hands with tapioca starch to prevent sticking. Take small portions of the dough and shape them into small balls, about the size of a golf ball.
11. Roll each ball into a thin rope, approximately 6-8 inches long. Join the ends of the rope to form a circle, shaping it into a rosca.

12. Place the shaped rosca on the prepared baking sheet, leaving some space between them.
13. Bake in the preheated oven for about 25-30 minutes, or until the rosca turns golden brown and slightly crispy on the outside.
14. Remove from the oven and let the rosca cool on a wire rack before serving.

Cuscuz de Tapioca

A popular northeastern Brazilian dessert made with tapioca pearls, coconut milk, and condensed milk.

Ingredients:

2 cups tapioca pearls (small or medium-sized)
2 cups coconut milk
1 cup whole milk
1 cup granulated sugar
1/2 cup shredded coconut (unsweetened)
1/2 cup condensed milk
1 tsp. vanilla extract
Pinch of salt
Fresh fruit for garnish (optional)

Directions:

1. Place the tapioca pearls in a large bowl and cover them with water.
2. Let them soak for about 1 hour, or until they become soft and translucent.
3. Drain the soaked tapioca pearls and set them aside.
4. In a saucepan, combine the coconut milk, whole milk, granulated sugar, shredded coconut, condensed milk, vanilla extract, and a pinch of salt.
5. Stir well to combine.
6. Place the saucepan over medium heat and bring the mixture to a simmer, stirring constantly to dissolve the sugar.
7. Gradually add the soaked tapioca pearls to the simmering milk mixture, stirring continuously.
8. Cook for about 5-7 minutes, or until the mixture thickens to a creamy consistency.
9. Remove the saucepan from the heat and let the cuscuz de tapioca cool slightly.
10. Lightly grease a round or rectangular mold with a little bit of vegetable oil.

11. Pour the tapioca mixture into the greased mold, pressing it down gently to make it compact.
12. Cover the mold with plastic wrap and refrigerate for at least 2 hours, or until the cuscuz is firm and set.
13. When ready to serve, carefully invert the mold onto a serving platter to release the cuscuz.
14. It should come out easily.
15. Garnish the cuscuz with fresh fruit if desired.
16. Slice and serve the Cuscuz de Tapioca chilled as a delightful and refreshing dessert.

Sopa Leão Veloso

A comforting soup made with beef, vegetables, and pasta, often served with a splash of vinegar and a sprinkle of grated cheese.

Ingredients:

1 lb beef, cubed
1 onion, finely chopped
2 cloves of garlic, minced
2 tbsps. vegetable oil
2 medium tomatoes, diced
2 medium carrots, diced
2 medium potatoes, diced
1 cup cabbage, shredded
4 cups beef broth
1 bay leaf
Salt and pepper to taste
Chopped parsley for garnish

Directions:

1. In a large pot, heat the vegetable oil over medium heat.
2. Add the onion and garlic, and sauté until the onion becomes translucent and the garlic is fragrant.
3. Add the beef cubes to the pot and brown them on all sides.
4. Stir in the diced tomatoes and cook for a few minutes until they start to soften.
5. Add the diced carrots, potatoes, and shredded cabbage to the pot.
6. Mix well to combine all the ingredients.
7. Pour in the beef broth and add the bay leaf. Season with salt and pepper to taste.
8. Bring the soup to a boil, then reduce the heat to low. Cover the pot and let the soup simmer for about 30-40 minutes, or until the beef and vegetables are tender.
9. Taste the soup and adjust the seasoning if needed.
10. Remove the bay leaf from the pot before serving.

11. Ladle the Leão Veloso Soup into bowls and garnish with chopped parsley.
12. Serve the soup hot and enjoy!

Mungunzá

A sweet porridge made with boiled corn kernels, coconut milk, sugar, and spices.

Ingredients:

1 cup dried white corn kernels (Mungunzá or Canjica)
4 cups water
1 cinnamon stick
4 cups coconut milk
1 cup granulated sugar
1 cup whole milk
Ground cinnamon for sprinkling (optional)

Directions:

1. Rinse the dried white corn kernels under running water to remove any impurities.
2. In a large pot, combine the corn kernels, water, and cinnamon stick. Bring to a boil over medium-high heat.
3. Reduce the heat to low and let the corn kernels simmer for about 1 to 2 hours, or until they become tender.
4. Stir occasionally to prevent sticking.
5. Once the corn kernels are tender, add the coconut milk, granulated sugar, and whole milk to the pot.
6. Stir well to combine.
7. Continue cooking over low heat, stirring occasionally, for about 30 minutes or until the mixture thickens to a creamy consistency.
8. Remove the pot from the heat and let the Mungunzá cool slightly.
9. Serve the Mungunzá warm in bowls, sprinkling ground cinnamon on top if desired.
10. Enjoy this delicious Brazilian dessert!

Angu à Baiana

A creamy polenta-like dish made from cornmeal, often served with a rich and spicy sauce made from dried shrimp, palm oil, and spices.

Ingredients:

1 cup yellow cornmeal
4 cups water
2 tbsps. vegetable oil
1 onion, finely chopped
2 cloves of garlic, minced
1 tomato, diced
1 bell pepper, diced
2 tbsps. fresh cilantro, chopped
Salt and pepper to taste

Directions:

1. In a medium saucepan, bring the water to a boil.
2. In a separate bowl, mix the yellow cornmeal with 1 cup of cold water until well combined and there are no lumps.
3. Slowly pour the cornmeal mixture into the boiling water, stirring continuously to avoid any lumps from forming.
4. Reduce the heat to low and let the mixture simmer for about 10-15 minutes, stirring occasionally, until the mixture thickens and the cornmeal is fully cooked.
5. In a separate pan, heat the vegetable oil over medium heat.
6. Add the chopped onion and minced garlic and sauté until they become translucent and fragrant.
7. Add the diced tomato and bell pepper to the pan and cook for a few minutes until they soften.
8. Pour the sautéed vegetables into the pot with the cooked cornmeal.
9. Stir well to combine.
10. Season with salt and pepper to taste and continue cooking for another 5 minutes to allow the flavors to meld.

11. Remove from heat and stir in the chopped fresh cilantro.
12. Serve the Angu à Baiana warm as a side dish or as a base for stews, sauces, or toppings.

Rocambole

A rolled cake filled with sweet fillings such as guava paste, dulce de leche, or chocolate.

Sponge Cake Ingredients:

4 large eggs
3/4 cup granulated sugar
1 cup all-purpose flour
1 tsp. baking powder
1/4 tsp. salt
1 tsp. vanilla extract

Filling Ingredients:

1 cup dulce de leche or your preferred filling (chocolate, fruit jam, etc.)

Directions:

1. Preheat your oven to 350°F (175°C). Grease a baking sheet and line it with parchment paper.
2. In a mixing bowl, beat the eggs and sugar together until they become light and fluffy.
3. In a separate bowl, whisk together the flour, baking powder, and salt.
4. Gradually add the dry ingredients to the egg mixture, folding gently with a spatula until well combined.
5. Stir in the vanilla extract.
6. Pour the batter onto the prepared baking sheet and spread it evenly to form a thin layer.
7. Bake in the preheated oven for about 10-12 minutes, or until the cake is lightly golden and springs back when touched.
8. While the cake is still warm, carefully remove it from the baking sheet and place it on a clean kitchen towel or parchment paper.
9. Spread the dulce de leche or your preferred filling evenly over the surface of the cake.

10. Starting from one edge, carefully roll the cake into a tight cylinder, using the towel or parchment paper to assist you. Roll it gently but firmly to prevent cracking.
11. Once rolled, transfer the rocambole to a serving platter or tray, seam side down.
12. Let it cool completely before slicing and serving.

About the Author

Laura Sommers is **The Recipe Lady!**

She lives on a small farm in Baltimore County, Maryland and has a passion for food. She has taken cooking classes in New York City, Memphis, New Orleans and Washington DC. She has been a taste tester for a large spice company in Baltimore and written food reviews for several local papers. She loves writing cookbooks with the most delicious recipes to share her knowledge and love of cooking with the world.

Follow her on Pinterest:

http://pinterest.com/therecipelady1

Visit the Recipe Lady's blog for even more great recipes:

http://the-recipe-lady.blogspot.com/

Visit her Amazon Author Page to see her latest books:

amazon.com/author/laurasommers

Follow the Recipe Lady on Facebook:

https://www.facebook.com/therecipegirl

Follow her on Twitter:

https://twitter.com/TheRecipeLady1

Other Books by Laura Sommers

Irish Recipes for St. Patrick's Day

Traditional Vermont Recipes

Traditional Memphis Recipes

Maryland Chesapeake Bay Blue Crab Cookbook

Mussels Cookbook

Maryland Chesapeake Bay Blue Crab Cookbook

Salmon Cookbook

Scallop Recipes

Printed in Great Britain
by Amazon

8bb47775-fcda-4643-b394-326c11e6b403R01